DUKES UP &

Faith For Every Round

A MEMOIR

DUKES UP &

Faith For Every Round

A MEMOIR

SHIMEKA DUKES

FAITH PLUS WORKS PUBLICATIONS

Printed in the United States of America
First Printing, 2020
ISBN 978-0-578-64993-1
Published by: Faith Plus Works Publications
dukesupbooks@gmail.com
www.dukesupbooks.com

Cover Design: DzineBK | www.dzinebk.com
Interior Design: Glory to Glory Publications, LLC |
www.WendiHayman.com

TABLE OF CONTENTS

IN THE DARK

ROUND 1

Childhood: Graham Cracker and Punch Buggy Days

ROUND 2

Puppy Love: The beginning of what I once considered first love

ROUND 3
Bereavement: Mourning Sun

ROUND 4
College: A Snore at the Student Union

ROUND 5
Love Hunt: A Heart without a Home

IN THE LIGHT

ROUND 6
Living Rich: Silver Spoon

ROUND 7
Unveiled: Out of the Closet

ACKNOWLEDGMENTS

Thy word is a lamp unto my feet and a light unto my path.
Psalms 119:105
King James Version (KJV)

I'd like to thank God (the Father), His son, my Lord and Savior (Jesus Christ) and the Holy Spirit for continuing to use me. I thank God for my mother, Jean K. Dukes. It was a chapter in mom's life that birthed this relaunch. Lastly, I would like to thank God for my mentor Tressa Azarel Smallwood. She is the midwife that pushed me relentlessly to deliver what God already had in store for me to birth. Thank you, Lord, for Your glory.

Keep the Faith in Jesus Mighty, Powerful & Strong Name,
Shimeka

Ding!

IN THE DARK

Dark (/därk/)

Adjective: dark; comparative adjective: darker; superlative adjective: darkest

1. with little or no light.

"it's too dark to see much"

2. (of a color or object) not reflecting much light; approaching black in shade.

"dark green"

Noun: dark; noun: the dark; plural noun: darks

1. the absence of light in a place.

"Carolyn was sitting in the dark"

2. a dark color or shade, especially in a painting.

I was IN THE DARK. Mentally – I was like Carolyn in the Oxford dictionary's example of how to use dark in a sentence when used as a noun. I was sitting in the dark. Sitting in the dark originally started while sitting in my bedroom and writing in my teenage diary from the age of fourteen to my mid-twenties (1994-2004). A few housekeeping items before we get started and get all deep! Disclaimer. I am a creative writer and a former closet writer. What does that mean and why would you care? As a creative writer, all my creativity and writing inspirations come from God. Secondly, being a former closet writer, means at times I purposely wrote extremely vague journal entries because I had no intent as a teenager to share the testimonies from my diary publicly. I mean, I made it my business to hide every single sheet of paper that came to life by these thoughts I stamped with an ink pen. As a result, it may be challenging at times to follow what I am conveying. Therefore, here are a few things to note for your sanity. Throughout the book I will reference my bedroom (my sacred place), as *"the closet"* and the pieces/journal entries from my diary as *"sheets"*. I was twenty-five years old before conceiving that I had sat in this place "in the dark" – a state of depression, for so long. For ten years I had isolated myself and wrote behind closed doors. My diary was my refuge. But I was wrong. I belonged to God way before teenage depression set in and Jesus was my ultimate refuge.

You see, in 1988, at the precious age of eight, I was baptized in a Baptist church. And while I knew in my heart that Jesus was real, there were periods in my teenage and young adult years when my faith in God shrunk smaller than a mustard seed. I had so many doubts, setbacks and disappointments. I had no appetite for life, and I was privately angry with and questioning God. Oh, yes! I know—crazy me! And yes, I'm sure you're thinking, ah! Now we're getting to the real meaning of *"closet sheets."* Well, after much reflection and deliverance from depression God revealed to me that each journal entry written down was a prayer. Basically, through my diary I was seeking him. Secondly, God answered every prayer that went forth and nothing will ever be too hard for Him. Problems come daily and every day is a new *"round,"* but the battle is not ours. The fight will get frustrating, but there is peace and we win when we fight by taking everything to the rock in Jesus mighty, powerful and strong name. Lastly, God revealed that when we seek Him and when we believe ("have faith"), He equips us and gives us the grace and the strength to endure on this journey called life, in both day ("the light") and night ("the darkness"). God's word is truly our daily bread.

So, what's in your closet? Who is the real you? Who knows the real you and everything about you? Your insecurities, your deepest secrets, your skeletons, your guilty pleasures and regrets? Don't worry. I'll be the last one to judge you. And, you'll never have to answer to me. However, if you're going to start *faith-ing it*, you are going to have to put in the hard work and self-examination is part of the process. It's time to get in the ring now. Don't be afraid. God's grace is ALWAYS enough.

Keep the Faith in Jesus Mighty, Powerful & Strong Name!
Ding!

ROUND 1

CHILDHOOD
Graham Cracker & Punch Buggy Days

He Knew Me?

Yes, Jesus knew (and knows) me! He knew me before and after I was born, and He knew you too!

I had an excellent childhood. You'll find that in the pieces that I wrote, I was reflecting on the good ole' days. We made our routine family car rides to Queens, New York, in the winter to see my dad's side of the family—my grandparents, aunt and first cousin. And we took family trips to LaGrange, Georgia, to see my mom's side of the family during the summer.

I have fond childhood memories of my only older brother and me playing hide and seek, jumping on the furniture, and building forts around the house. I treasure the memories of the day I was baptized, as well as going to church on homecoming Sunday and weekly for mom and dad's choir rehearsal.

Third Floor, Please

In loving memory of my Uncle Wesley
Written August 1994

My father's best friend
His only brother
He would always laugh
He would always chuckle
This nice young man was Wesley
My uncle

When times were good
When times were bad
My uncle I knew
I always had

"How are you doing?"
Just saying, "I'm fine" won't do
Uncle wanted us to be marvelous,
Super or fantastic
To pass through

Not just his door

But life, live full
Grandpa, he was not careless
Like you harmlessly joked
He was caring and inspirational
He was wonderful

He called cousin, Jenny, "Bunny Rabbit"
He said she ate anything,

But carrot sticks

He called my brother, Al, "Pumpkin"
Because he ate good too
Always entertaining the family with weird stunts
Only Al considered tricks

Uncle called me "Sistah"
With no strings attached
Among the rabbit and the pumpkin
I was the different one in the patch

I recall jumping on his exercise bike
As he gave me "don't hurt yourself" looks
And I was so fascinated
By his fifty plus JET
Black Entertainment books

I remember my uncle
In various ways
No one could describe him
Like I have today

I remember my uncle's gestures
And his smiling face
Among all the best
He'd never be replaced

I remember my uncle
From the very start
For he's the painter of this art
I miss him

And will always love him
From the bottom of my heart

Daddy, I Still Remember
Written October 2000

I remember sitting with you
In a one-person chair
Disagreeing
With the referee of the Knick's basketball game
With great sportsmanship, yelling
"Come On"
"Are you kidding me?"
"That's not fair!"

I remember the rhythm
Of your strong and steady heartbeat
And, "Shimeka"
"Where are your slippers?"
"Why aren't they on your feet?"

"Zip up that coat daddy bought you
and where's your winter hat?"
"Put on your red turtleneck"
"You can't stay warm in just that!"

I remember how important family
gatherings were to you
A zillion trips to the archives in D.C.
There you were consistently
studying the family tree

"Hey"
"One of your cousins might be
Wesley Snipes" "Or Oprah"

"One of our extended aunts is the mother of
Muhammad Ali"

We traveled from Orlando to Detroit
Indiana to Petersburg
LaGrange to New York, NY
We bought boxes of cream soda
And ordered bags of White Castle's
cheeseburgers and onion rings
But no one could pay you to eat pork

I remember the kind words you said to
strangers you passed in the street
While Mom, Al and I waited patiently in the van
What we inaccurately complained
Was at least 90 degrees heat

I remember you by my side
On the sidewalks of Brook Drive
Riding my long-seated purple bike
I thought I was the luckiest kid alive
Reminding me to forget
The training
wheels were off,
Unknowingly
As your hand was no longer in sight
I began to ride independently
Oh, what a lesson for life

I remember the gigantic bowl of
Pretzels, popcorn and chips
You loved UTZ plain potato chips

I must admit,
They are the best without dip

I miss the days I pouted
And you made me give you
A hug and a kiss on the cheek

You can still call me "sistah"
Like uncle Wesley used to
Or even call me "Meke-Meke"
I'm still the little girl you knew back then
That drew pictures with chalk up and down our street
Here I am
Look up here
I've just grown a couple feet!

Me & Al, My Favorite Pal
A childhood memory
Written November 2000

Oh how I was scared
Of that piano tune
In the movie,
Halloween
And Jason with that hockey mask
Just his presence made me scream

Me and Al

Don't forget Freddie
From that street they called Elm
How did all these serial killers murder everyone?
They walked
They never ran

Me and Al

But I didn't have to worry
Al sat by me and held my hand
He reassured me that there was no such thing as a
Jason, Freddy or a Boogie Man

Me and Al
When the street lights came on
We had to depart from our playmates and go home
But for Al and I
Because we had each other the fun was never over
And we never played alone

There we were watching "The Last Dragon"
At approximately 8:00 PM
Like good little children
While daddy got his rest in

But before "Leroy" lit up with a yellow glow
Guess who's jumping couch to couch
Imitating the Superman show?

Me and Al

Who dumped all of the toys out of the toy barrel
To play Big Bird and Oscar the Grouch?
And who built the biggest forts out of Mom's best blankets
Only for Dad to shout?

Me and Al

Who has a bond that's tight for life?
And who is the best looking sister and brother on
Brook with a big rump they can't hide?
Well, other than Mrs. Dukes…

ME and AL!

The Boy I Admired from Afar
Written November 2000

There was this boy I knew
Three years older than me
Who told jokes so funny
He had you laughing hysterically

He was tall and skinny
He thought he was buff
Had thousands of scars because
Like most boys
He played rough

Girls loved and favored him
For his eyes were hazel
But what they didn't know
Was that he often left the toilet seat up
And rarely wiped off the kitchen table

In high school he played football
And in wrestling
Oh, he was the BEST
Check all the local newspaper companies or ask him
He'll put you in a move that will tell the rest!

Today he has a little girl
A spitting image of him perfectly
She'll be tall like him and as he was then...
Skinny
Today he is a little chunky

Today I realized
That the boy I admired from afar
Encouraged me to succeed
And is definitely my star

All of his accomplishments
More to mention indeed
Determined me more and more
To find ways to also succeed

To admire in this way again
There will never be any other
For that boy I knew
Who is now a man
Is also known as my brother

We Celebrate You

*A birthday wish to my
grandfather Albert J. Dukes, Sr.
Written April 2007*

A boy scout of America
The youngest child of a family of ten
It was April 23, 1917
When your ROUND did begin…
We celebrate you

Born in Arkansas
A place we are told called Roe
Throughout your lifetime held several positions
But not limited to
A barber, chef, mechanic, driver
And in 1942
Husband to Lillie O…
We celebrate you

Recipient of the WWII Bronze Star
Member of the United States Navy
United States Armed Services
And soldier of God's Army
You are…
We celebrate you

Former member of Calvary Baptist Church, NYC
For several years
You know
Served in the gospel choir
According to Albert Jr.

The Quartet pitch
Your best note…
We celebrate you

A root you are
In our family tree
An outstanding
Brother
Father
Grandfather

Great-Grandfather
Our honoree…
We celebrate you

We celebrate your
Past
We celebrate your
Today
With these words we extend
Our deepest love your way

WE CELEBRATE YOU
And wish you
A happy
And blessed
90th birthday

FAITH CORNER

In Jeremiah 1:5, I learned that the blueprint for my purpose in life is already mapped by the Creator.

Before I formed thee in the belly I knew thee and before thou cometh forth out of the womb I sanctified thee...
King James Version (KJV)

Have you asked the Creator about the blueprint for your purpose? He wants to hear from you!

PRAYER CORNER

_____

_____

_____

_____

_____

_____

_____

_____

_____

_____

_____

_____

_____

_____

_____

_____

_____

_____

_____

_____

_____

_____

_____

_____

_____

_____

Amen! Keep the Faith in Jesus Mighty, Powerful & Strong Name!
Next Round!

ROUND 2

PUPPY LOVE
The beginning of what I once considered first love.

He Loved Me?

Yes, Jesus loved (and loves) me! Okay, who remembers passing notes in class: "Do you love me? Circle yes or no."

Yeeeeessss! Life was so simple back then, right? Well, that's what this chapter is about. That l-u-v, not the real thang, l-o-v-e! That love that hurts so deep, and then you learn twenty-five years later that it was nothing near the real thing and if only you had known it back then!

I Never Thought
Written February 1996

I never thought
Someone as fine as you
Would want to get involved
With a girl like me

It was a birthday wish
Never thought of
There you were
My first love

You gave me respect
Pleasure
And most of all love

You were all I ever dreamed of
Together on your birth date
We would be

I never thought
Someone as fine as you
Would want to get involved
With a girl like me

You called me everyday
Asking me wus up
Of course
I only thought of you
So I had to make something up

When the phone call was over
It was completed with three strong words
My emotions were touched
And began to start
Those three words went straight to my heart

I never thought
Someone as fine as you
Would want to get involved
With a girl like me

Our communication ended
For a short while
Because a payment was overdue
My heart was burdened
I hadn't heard from my boo

Having fears and nightmares
That you found someone new
I was thinking of every negative situation
That I knew you wouldn't do

Losing my trust in you
Feeling you were fake
I was delighted with a kiss
From someone else
It was a huge mistake

This mistake led our relationship to an end
I was losing not only my first love
But my best friend

You forgave me
But will never forget
Now we hardly talk
And argue over nonsense

My heart is wounded
I guess I hurt you first
Now I'm without my first love
I'm getting what I deserve

All I do is have flashbacks
Like things you said to me on the phone
That made me wept
Like the first kiss you gave me
Like when we first met

Like our first laugh together
Like when we first fought
Like our trip to the playground and
Ride on the teeter-tots

Like our first apology
Like when I first cried
Like wondering if you still cared
Like wondering if you lied

I never thought you could hurt me mentally
Though you bragged you could physically
I never thought you would make me weak
I never thought we would be over so quickly

I never thought I would miss you
When you don't miss me

I still love you
That
I never thought
Would be a mistake

Not Once, But Twice
Written October 1996

I thought it was the same argument
Petty and plain
But when you said goodbye
I knew things would change

I set myself up
To be hurt again
Not one time but twice
In my mind
You had to be
The number one person in my life

My heart was broken
But now it's crushed
How can one give another
So much trust?

I have no words
But so much stress
How could he be
So different from the rest

If once wasn't enough
Twice probably won't do
But how many times
Will I get hurt
Because I love you?

Everything Happens for a Reason
Written May 2000

I've always said
Everything happens for a reason
But right now
I can't see the meaning

I saw you where I always do
In the middle of the crowd
Where some non-prospect was dancing behind me
Hoping and wishing it would be you

You show very little emotion
Which is tearing me apart
If you would just let me know what you want
I could begin to mend your heart

I can tell that you've been hurt
And you're craving more than
Physical pleasure
I'm willing to let you possess
What I consider valuable treasure

A treasure
Which is neither physical nor sexual
But a treasure
To be found you must travel the distance
To discover

But every time I think you take a step forward
It's actually three steps back

Please stop playing with my emotions
Once I've been turned away
I will not glare back

There's something pulling me to you
And though my legs and feet are numb
With you there's no hesitation
And I'm starting to feel where your words come from

Have your words been whispering all along?
And now decided to speak aloud?
Have they derived from the same fragile place?
The same which all I give to you have come from?

I can see it in your eyes
You're hurting like I am
I see drops fall and run over
Your eye
Though I've never seen you cry

Please
Let your guard down
And stop trying to hide
What I can see is already exposed

Lay with me
Not under the sheets
But with my thought and care

For
Everything happens for a reason
And that's why you and I were there

FAITH CORNER

I found God's love in John 3:16.

For God so loved the world, that he gave his one and only begotten son,
that whosoever believeth in him should not perish, but have
everlasting life.
King James Version (KJV)

Jesus loves you too. Seek Him diligently and you will feel his loving presence deep in your heart.

PRAYER CORNER

_____

_____

_____

_____

_____

_____

_____

_____

_____

_____

_____

_____

_____

_____

_____

_____

_____

_____

_____

_____

_____

_____

_____

_____

_____

_____

_____

Amen! Keep the Faith in Jesus Mighty, Powerful & Strong Name!
Next Round!

ROUND 3

BEREAVEMENT
Mourning Sun

He Comforted Me?

Yes, Jesus comforted (and comforts) me. We all will experience times in life when we will grieve the loss of a loved one. It is one of the toughest parts of life that never gets easier with experience.

Journal entries during this period of my life reflect my confusion, questions and responses to the deaths of classmates and family members. But I am so thankful to God for His son, Jesus, who died for you and me...the ultimate sacrifice, that we (through Him) may have everlasting life.

The phone is ringing. It's the bad news call.

To My Dear Friend
Written October 1996

We knew each other for years
But it seemed like a few
Elementary
Junior High
Senior High School too

You suffered for a while
But now you've gone away
To be with our heavenly father
You can rest better today

Though we weren't very close
Your friends were mine too
And all of us together
Will always be thinking of you

You were with us yesterday
And though you're gone today
The good times we shared
And memories of you
Will never ever stray

At Times
Written December 1999

At times it seems
As if all those I knew
Are slowly
Slipping away

They all passed by me yesterday
But many footprints
Have ceased today

Yes, a day
Will come for us all
Yet, there's one thing troubling me
And in the way

Why those straight from high school
Why those under age
Please forgive me
Not saying that rest is only for the gray

I will always remember your face
Especially your many jokes
But due to your depart
Parts of my laughter and joy
Are now broke

My heart is overwhelmed with pain
My mind is very confused
And I'll never understand why
Now was the time to choose

My Grandma Lillie
Written July 2001

She was kind and very sweet
A smiling face
Comforting spirit
Kept everything tidy and oh so neat
My grandma Lillie

[I recall her saying something of the sort]

"Hi Jeanie"
"You and Ms. Meka look so pretty"
"Let me call Jennie Pooh and Mary Lee"
"Papa, stop talking so crazy!"
"Here little Al, give your father this fifty."
My Grandma Lillie

Talked highly and praised
The successful, family and our Savior,
The Almighty
Put others before her
A hard worker
No time to be feisty
My grandma Lillie

Stocked in her cabinets
loads of grape jelly Just for me
No one could even persuade me
to eat those hominy grits
Only she

My grandma Lillie

She loved to have Deja
My niece
In her company
And was tickled by her presence

Now a great-grandmother
And proud grandmother of three
My grandma Lillie

She left the month of my birthday
I think she knew all along
For she talked of going to a place
And by the tone of her voice
There was no harm

I know she's looking down on us
She and Uncle Wes
She's probably saying,
"Live your life, stop all that fuss,
I left this place quietly"
"God knew what was bes'"

The smile we remember
And those helping hands that
Held the family together
Was that of a strong woman
Forever a missing link
Lillie
My grandmother

Don't Cry For Me

Inspired by "Rock the Boat,"
by the late R&B artist Aaliyah
Written November 2001

When I die
Like most request
Don't cry for me

Death
I did not know
Was approaching
I'm glad I wasn't informed
By a doctor
Telegram
Or sting

Though I leave behind
Written documents
That reflect much pain
Know that I lived a joyful life
Before and after the drizzle turned to rain

I will miss physically being with family, loved ones
And friends
But we'll see each other again one day soon
Maybe the next time you get a chill
It will be me passing through the wind
Or traveling back from the moon

In case I run out of time to tell
I do have one wish

Someone please
With the best of all the poems I've written
Attempt to publish

And if life doesn't keep you too busy
We can reminisce
About the good memories
While sipping on some of
my Mother's iced tea
Just as long as you promise
That when I die
Like many request
Please
Don't cry for me

FAITH CORNER

God provided me comfort at all times. Comfort was
found in II Corinthians 1:3 and II Corinthians 12:9.

Blessed be God, even the father of our Lord Jesus Christ, the father of
mercies and God of all comfort.
II Corinthians 1:3 (King James Version)

And he said unto me, my grace is sufficient for thee;
for my strength is made perfect in weakness.
II Corinthians 12:9 (King James Version)

God will comfort you. Have you asked Him for peace in the midst of your storm?

PRAYER CORNER

_____

_____

_____

_____

_____

_____

_____

_____

_____

_____

_____

_____

_____

_____

_____

_____

_____

_____

_____

_____

_____

_____

_____

_____

_____

_____

Amen! Keep the Faith in Jesus Mighty, Powerful & Strong Name!
Next Round!

ROUND 4

COLLEGE
A Snore at the Student Union

Please Sustain Me.

Yes, Jesus sustained (and sustains) me. I was eight years old when Spike Lee's film, *School Daze*, hit the streets! I had no clue then that ten years later, I too would be attending a historically black college.

This chapter of my life captures my expressions while enrolled at an HBCU. I'm going to be honest: I was on an emotional roller coaster during my college years - but thank God for the church.

Equally, this chapter reveals my transition to a career in corporate America. Let me tell you somethin' (in my aunt Mary's voice, God rest her soul)—both were a different world! Most importantly, in addition to these changes and transitions, I noticed in hindsight that there was also a spiritual shifting taking place.

There was a shift from questions of doubt to making specific requests known to God through my prayers (journaling). Everything that I wrote still went under the bed, but I was getting stronger—slowly, but surely.

A Feeling
Written January 1997

A feeling that comes and goes
A feeling that tries
A feeling that will never die

It brings you down
It tears you away
It feels like winter
The month after May

A feeling that comes and goes
A feeling that tries
A feeling that will never die

It hurts like hell
Though you'll never tell
Inside your body
It will swell

A feeling that comes and goes
A feeling that tries
A feeling that will never die

It will bring you misery
And replace all cheer
With overflowing tears...
Pain

Luckily, No Proof
Written February 2000

I can't explain
What I'm going through
I have no evidence
I have no proof

I'm not even talking about love
What I question is,
Is he being true?

Are the words that roll off his tongue
Sincere
Or does his tongue
Do all the sincere talking

Or has it been too long
For the right one for me
And that I've simply had no options

We are only considered "friends"
So how can I get disturbed?
Possibly because of what I've seen too many times
Not what he thinks I've probably heard

I say I don't want a relationship
But just between my heart and I
That is definitely a lie
But he who is the one for me
Could tell by looking in my eyes

I told myself
I would be prepared next time
But no matter what
Precaution I take
Something always tells me to stay

Is it truly?
The whisper of my heart
Telling me not to stray?
Because it's starting to sound like
The same whisper
That pushed my last love away

I try not to connect the pieces
I hope I don't get a clue
Because I sense the feeling I had
With my last love
But luckily, I have no proof

Relief, Not Grief

I'll Never Again Have to Wonder "What if"
Written 2000

I've come to the conclusion
That you can't make someone love you
No matter how true you are
Though there are many beautiful qualities you possess
He may never notice them
Or it may be too late when he does

You love him for who he is
Or what he wants to be
Not for the finer opportunities
And you are blind to any of his flaws
Or shortcomings

You even gave him a second chance
Or more...
But don't kick yourself in the rear
Just proudly strut out the door

He may have taken my time
Even tried to boggle my mind
But he has no choice to remember
My individual style
Empathy
Words of encouragement
Strength
Energy

Most of all
Our moments
And yes
It was all worthwhile!

To a Friend of Mine

In response to a friend's emergency
Written November 2000

I'm left alone in the dark
The only thing I hear...
Is the cry of my heart
Why did this happen
When did it start?
Lord, if you can hear me
Please make it stop

Though I heard no whispers
And my eyes were closed shut
Though no one responded to the knocks
The door opened up

At one point
I'm afraid to walk in
At another
I'm dying to go
But what if inside lies a secret
I'd rather not know

I may not know what's happening to you
I respect your privacy
I just wanted to let you know
I'm praying for you
Stay strong
With yours truly
That is me...
Shimeka

The Anonymous D
A French Chef
Written December 2000

Girl
He blows my mind with the words he says
The way he expresses himself
Sometimes in French
He's so convincing
This love thing hurts my head
Is he Mr. Right?
Or just Mr. Right Now?

Should I play him like a joker
Or should I play my hand?
He's as persistent as the mailman
The weather report
Girl, huh
Even your menstrual cycle hasn't been more on point
But one minute I enjoy it
Another I don't

He calls 2-3 times a day
A fourth just to say goodnight
I know he better slow down
I'm starting to like this play
Playa I hope he's not

We've spent some time together
I hope it's not all a joke
But girl, I'll call you tomorrow
Because until time passes by
I'll never know

Strangers, Even Enemies, More Kind Than Friends
Written May 2001

Paint the picture of what you want me to see
Go ahead
Pick all the poisonous apples
From your tree

But with the season
You will involuntarily define
What you are and trying to hide
The entire time

Your other half is going insane
The revised you
Is screaming time out
I want out of the game

Surprisingly
You're not even a friend to yourself
You are a thief in the night
You are a splinter in a shelf

Trust self-vision
For it's not impaired
It's evident this crook
Has taken his share

Smile at your enemies
Be kind to your kin
Always caution to those persons

That you label your friend

Like the Wind
Written September 2001

Fear to make a friend
Fear to be me
Like the wind
Oh, could it be

One second you hear it whisper
And in a minute
It is gone

In the summer
Particularly late August, on a place
Such as on the beach
It's soothing, comforting, and quite a charm

But by autumn, mid-September
It's fading, slowly passing
Not even knowing it does harm

And in a minute
It's gone
Stripped by rhetoric
Like a naked tree
The wind manipulated every branch
And limb
Until it was done
Cruel, but familiar intension
And in a minute
It was gone

In less than fourteen days there was union
Frequently
Four times within four weeks
It was we
The wind and me

But in a month and three weeks
There was silence
The tree had lost its leaves

Then there was a moan
Not from you
But I
And like the wind
In a minute
We were gone

Seasons with Invisible Change
Written September 2001

You changed with the season
I'll never really know why
Is it because you are a "man"
A redundant, sorry, somehow inherited excuse
The only claim upon
Which I can rely

I thought you had to be hurt
At least once
To know or have reason to play the game
But just like a pro
You Like others
Called quits and did the same

For once I had found one up to my
So called "Standards"
Had ambition, a career and more than one goal
What I admired most was your affection
And lack of fear to put me in your arms
To hug and hold

But the fear you did possess
You would never tell
That's why you're heart, this long, has been well
Or is it?
Does it swell?

Anytime
Any day

When you are ready to be the man
We already give you respect and acknowledge to be

Give me the real reason
Because my heart
Will always speak the same
No matter the season

Pain All Around Me
Written October 2001

Pain can be like the ocean
It's forever all around me

Holding my breath
Fighting not to drown
Every now and then
A wave of joy comes around

I search and hope for land
From sun up to down
But as soon as I reach the top
The surface beneath me turns to sinking sand

I've had enough dirt
I've tasted enough salt
I'm tired of struggling
I just want to walk

I have to keep on going
I'll have to cough and choke
For tomorrow I may float
If I'm lucky
I'll cruise in a boat

To Be or Not to Be
Written November 2001

To be in the light
Or in the shadow
Rags or riches
Platinum or gold
Kisses or disses
Lied to or told

Highest bidder
Or item sold
Misses or mistress
The youth
Or the old

Ugly on the exterior
Beauty only within
Or vice versa
Black as the pavement
Light as gin

Salt or pepper
Bitter or sweet
Truthful and caring
Heartless or not a cheat

Vegetables or meat
Admired or ashamed
Given a label
Or called
Ms. your last name

Wild or tame

Dr. Phil
Dr. Feel Good
Or Driving Ms. Insane

Fantasy or fiction
Crime blamed on television programs
Not the life of hustler cousin Joe
His crack addict mother
And life on project lane

It's life
Not a game
With two opposing sides
Or could it be?
Someone call time out
And tell me

Because regardless of
What I did yesterday
If I fail
Lose
Or quit
What I've done this far
Doesn't mean a bit

Professor "Trust Me"
A Tribute to a Professor
Written January 2002

A comedian or instructor
To entertain or educate
Thank God this class is an elective
Not a requirement for me to graduate

Your heart means well
Keep laughing or fail
Pick up your head
I need you to stay awake
Let's talk about my nephew
Cousin Ju-Ju
And my uncle
Uncle Tate

Five days a week
Nine to four I work
Then five to nine class
Did I eat?
Quit the free counseling sessions
I can stay at home
I'm beat!

When is the take home?
Or open book exam
No need to cheat
I respect you as an elder
And love you to death
But stick to the book or dismiss class
Because I am tired of this mess!

Insomnia Statistic
Written February 2002

Thank you, Mr. El Dorado
And self
For today I experience
A consequence
No longer a fraction of the slim 1.4 percent

A lesson I thought
I'd learned before
Once again
I knocked on the wrong neighbor's door

A promise kept
I did not
A regret
No
A story must be told

A testimony
Another of life's lessons sought
Oh Lord,
If you please forgive me once more

Guide me and provide me with
A new start
This I ask
And confess
Straight from my heart

FAITH CORNER

Psalms 139:1-10 King James Version (KJV)
confirmed that no matter my mood or
situation, I learned that God knows all about it and is
always with me. Father, I thank you for wrapping me in
your arms.

O Lord, thou hast searched me, and known me. Thou knowest
my down-sitting and my uprising, though understandest
my thought afar off. Thou compass my path and my lying
down, and art acquainted with all my ways. For there is
not a word in my tongue, but, lo, O Lord, thou knowest it
all together. Thou has beset me behind and before, and laid
thine hand upon me. Such knowledge is too wonderful for
me; it is high, I cannot attain unto it. Whither shall I go
from thy spirit? Or wither shall I flee from thy presence? If
I ascend up into heaven, thou art there: if I make my bed
in hell, behold, thou art there. If I take the wings of the
morning, and dwell in the uttermost parts of the sea; Even
there shall thy lead me, and thy right hand shall hold me.

God knows everything about you, so no need to try to hide it from Him. Ask Him for help.

PRAYER CORNER

_____

_____

_____

_____

_____

_____

_____

_____

_____

_____

_____

_____

_____

_____

_____

_____

_____

_____

_____

_____

_____

_____

_____

_____

_____

Amen! Keep the Faith in Jesus Mighty, Powerful & Strong Name!
Next Round!

ROUND 5

LOVE HUNT
A Heart without a Home

Please Lead Me.

Yes, Jesus led (and leads) me. You know that saying, "Almost doesn't count"? Well, this describes how I was feeling at this point in my life.

Brothers never, barely, or almost did whatever I expected. I "almost" hung out with someone. I "almost" went on a real date. I "almost received a phone call back. He "almost" wanted me to meet his mother. He was "almost" over his ex-girlfriend, with her shoes still in the closet and her picture, around his neck.

I think you get the point. And guess what? I ALMOST gave up. But God! Thank you, Jesus, for leading me and guiding me as I searched for love.

Never
Written November 1998

I just knew I couldn't get hurt
By him twice
Did he really hurt me?
Or did I hurt myself

I keep telling myself
The pain will soon go away
But actually
It never strays

How long will it take?
Pieces of my heart
When I find another?
When I die?
When?

I will never get close to another
I have no choice but to push away
But then how will I ease the pain
I have now that won't go away

I'm very confused
It's tearing me apart
Mentally
I'm damaged
Never to love again

An Experience I Longed For
Written December 2000

I want to experience laughing
Until I can't laugh anymore
I want to live life
Like a hobby
Not a chore

I want to experience smiling
Because I'm happy
Not as a part of my facade
I want it to be indescribable
Abnormal or odd

I want to experience being
Hypnotized
By two eyes
Not blinded by
Weakness
Fear or lies

I want to feel high
Without a sip of Alize or Paul Mason
I want to be appreciated
Not intimidating or interrogated
For things
I've done

I want to be completely comfortable
With a stranger
Rather than busy

Sharpening my mental knife
or loading my mental gun

I want to celebrate life
And not worry
About when I die
I want to play
And dream like an innocent child

Be respectable and responsible
But also have time to be wild
I want the feelings I possess
To glow on the outside
Like the stars above
What I want to experience...
Is this thing
Called
Love

A Woman Scorned

Inspired by a single dad
Written June 2001

I cried last night
A cause
I don't why

The air is hot
Air conditioner working
It is not

Paid strangers
Ring the phone off the hook
Concrete, Benches, Sidewalks
A home
I avoid to look

Friend
Lover
Homie-Lover-Friend
What is this dead trend?

Lots of lust
To repent
I must

No room for trust
Rosa Parks I thank you
Like the back of a bus
Too dark

To focus
Is tough
Like the lack of light
There's no
Such thing as us

I get a high from your
Cheer
Emotion
Laugh
Smile
Wait...
Suggested creeps only after dark?
When baby momma is on duty
Or away 300 plus mile?

Jill Scott
I feel you
But she IS in
the way
Or maybe I'm in the way
Either way
This never started affair
Ends today

Had me on the side
Like red beans and rice
When I'm worth a bucket
Of breast,
leg and thigh
Plus a crisp apple pie

I didn't need you
You just killed my time
Instead I could have been rockin with Big G
BYB always makes me party and mingle

I hear their remix,
"Girl you look ...why don't you..."
So what if I'm shaped like a number eight
Or as I've been told like a Coca-Cola bottle
Don't hate
Yes, I'm only 21
And I am also single

Much respect to Maya Angelou
But Phenomenal
Isn't the description for
Women of 2001
If you ask
Some of the men where I'm from

Neither is "Ay shortay
When I'm 5'8 tall
"Ay Psucos"
Stop it
The stretch jeans I'm wearing
Are definitely Milan

"Ay You"
When I was born with a name
Shouted out by surprisingly
Confident nobodies
Even old heads

Which is pretty lame

Ladies keep hope alive
It's summer time
In the DC metro area
And I'm not going to front or jive

Barbecues, the Unity Fest with Chuck
It's live
Four to Five
I might find...
Well
Losers

Hmmm High School Diploma
Or your GED
Almost finished my
College degree
And it's still not WE
Just single
Black and me

Currently without employment
But hey I'm still in school
Though I don't have a man
I date whomever
"I" choose

Though most see me as happy and humorous
Like anyone
From time to time
I sing the blues

So dang it
Why did I cry last night?
An answer
I cannot give you

Miles Traveled Too Far: Love's Scar
Written January 2002

On the bottom of
Shoe soles
The shadow
Of a hole

A tunnel
Without light
A gear-less
Seat-less
Or one-wheeled bike

A penny
A lower case (j) in Jenny
Less
When you expect many

A sun without rise
A cloud without a sky
Flip flops without feet
A beach without
Surrounding sea

A debate
Without a discussion
All lost
As if I put in nothing
Twenty-one years past my hometown
But the place I circled round and round

What is it that caused me to travel
Thus far
The dust is clearing
It's Love's scar

Refuse to Let Me Stray
Written August 2002

I refuse to insist you stay
As a result of guilt
Or persuasion

Love in return
From you
I rather begin another of life's
Round and a day

Hurt
Not because of lies
But because of fear and time
Loose strands
Of the emotional tie

Your love for me
Exposed under the white light
Far before mine for you
Hidden under limbs of my shadowed tree

All of a sudden
My dreams became a reality
Joy
Nightmare
Episode
In one breathe

The man whom loved me first
Communicated through sweet actions

And gestures
Worth more to me
Than meaningless words
Awaited me to claim his heart

I did
But never told
Fear that confession
Would draw us apart
And watched our chances unfold

Today
Another love of the few
Gone
But I chose to Stray
Always
I will remember you
A price
I will have to pay

To be sure you chose to love me
And was not forced my way
I refuse to insist you stay

I refuse to admit I love you
Instead
I'll pray
You'll refuse to allow me to leave you alone
Another life's round
And a day

Dear Love
Written November 2002

Love

As we grow
No longer as simple as
Do you like me?
Circle yes or no

With time a combination
Both love, lust and hate
Hopeless thinking
And an underlying faith

A vision of perfection
Magnified with defect
A vision of lovemaking as a result of
Non-verbal emotion
Not just an instant effect

Maturity due to the mind
Not age
Reunion despite a phase of
Confusion, denial, transition and rain
In departure
I...
No we
Share a glimpse of the insane

Out
But back in

My life
You had to be

This time around
Like a stroll in the park
Let's talk and walk
But on our tip toe
With caution
Like a walk on broken glass
Or hot coal
To make it last

Out
But back in
Never again
To let go
Because true love to find
Will never be as simple as
Do you like me?
Circle yes or no

FAITH CORNER

There is no greater love than God's love and the love of Jesus Christ.
Through the reading of John 14, I strive to be worry-free,
for I know God cares.

Let your heart not be troubled, ye believe in God, believe also in me.
John 14:1 King James Version (KJV)

What is worrying you? Have you submitted your concerns to God?

PRAYER CORNER

_____

_____

_____

_____

_____

_____

_____

_____

_____

_____

_____

_____

_____

_____

_____

_____

_____

_____

_____

_____

_____

_____

_____

_____

_____

_____

_____

Amen! Keep the Faith in Jesus Mighty, Powerful & Strong Name!
Next Round!

IN THE LIGHT

Light (/līt/)

Noun: light

1. the natural agent that stimulates sight and makes things visible.
   "the light of the sun"

2. an expression in someone's eyes indicating a particular emotion or mood.
   "a shrewd light entered his eyes"

Verb: light; 3rd person present: lights; past tense: lit; gerund or present participle: lighting; past participle: lighted

1. provide with light or lighting; illuminate.
   "the room was lighted by a number of small lamps"

2. make (something) start burning; ignite.
   "Allen gathered sticks and lit a fire"

Adjective: light; comparative adjective: lighter; superlative adjective: lightest

1. having a considerable or sufficient amount of natural light; not dark.
   "the bedrooms are light and airy"

2. of a color) pale.
   "her eyes were light blue"

In the Light

You, Lord, are my lamp;
the Lord turns my darkness into light.
2 Samuel Chapter 22:9 New International Version (NIV)

I was CHANGING. Like David, the Lord was delivering me. God was delivering me from my darkness. In December 2005, I came out of the closet and didn't even know it. I exposed my sacred diary, my sheets, my prayers to God and didn't even know it! I shared a portion (just a sheet; just a piece, y'all) of the gift God gave to me that I had been hiding under my bed all of those years, even before internalizing that it was a gift, and my life has been forever—and I mean FOR-EVER—changed. I continued to write in 2006, but something was happening. My journal entries were different. My questions turned to affirmations; my faith trampled fears and closed doors; my ears, eyes and heart opened, and I went from writing in the darkest darkness into writing in His sacred light.

Today, I present to you more than just another book on the shelf. I give to you the gift God gave to me—the power of faith, prayer and testimony through journaling. My prayer is that through this gift, my journey and the reflections on paper that accumulated over the years, that you too have and will continue to experience the Lord's presence and revelation and that you chase after Him always and be obedient to the calling on your life and the gifts that He desires to bestow on you.

Keep the Faith in Jesus Mighty, Powerful & Strong Name!

Ding!

ROUND 6

LIVING RICH
Silver Spoon

He Freed Me!

Yes, He freed (frees) me. Lord, I can't thank you enough. It's about revelation, followed by restoration and living in an unfamiliar place called peace. Revelation from past mental bondage. A major turning point in my faith. Rich in mind, body and soul. It's about becoming a new creature with a new spirit and new lenses.

Far from and by no means perfect, but full of faith and forgiveness through your grace and mercy for yourself and others. I can't thank you enough. Thank you, Jesus, for the many sheets of paper; the prayers that you led me to write down in the closet, in the dark, and hidden under the bed—for your glory. Amen.

A Journey
Written December 2001

When I left my home
I was no longer a kid
I was grown...
So I thought
Of course
There was much of the unknown

I walked the walk
And tried to talk the talk
But after a couple of miles
I realized
I am still a child
And interestingly
I didn't mind

The world is much different
When you are thought of as an adult
You may think it is luxury
But it is also quite tough

Today is the day
That many have looked forward to
Some are here to witness
Others have been called away

But without all of the support
My round wouldn't have
Been complete
So I thank you all

I take my hat off
To the end of the heat

Now I can return home
In the same flesh and tan
But this time without a doubt
I'm no longer a child
But a woman

The New Year
Written January 2002

With a pop of champagne
You get a glimpse of
Sunshine
And rain

To forgive but not forget
Forget not forgive
Is all the same
What will I avoid
This time?
To make a change

A time to rejoice
A time to make a choice
A time for cheer
And forget or face all fear

With praise
Wine
Beer
Or a tear
Count the seconds down
For it's a new year!

The Significance of Life's Tense:
My Past and My Present
Written January 2002

Yesterday I frowned
Today I smile
Yesterday I took one step
Today I'll run a mile

Yesterday I was old
Today I'm young
Yesterday I drank E&J
Today it may be Bacardi Rum

Yesterday I cried
Today I laugh
Yesterday I was below average
in Algebra and Geometry
Today I have a 4.0
In math

Yesterday I made a wish
Today I pursue a long-term goal
Yesterday I didn't shave my legs
Or comb my hair
Today I pay for someone to paint my nails
And my toes

Yesterday I had a paper cut
And thought I'd surely die on my couch
Today I fell
Tripped

And bumped my head
And didn't even say ouch

For yesterday
Was the past
And my today
Is now

Wings of a Dream
Written February 2002

Support can make a dream
Whether you wish to
Travel to mars
Or a beach
The short distance an apple
may fall from its native tree

Suddenly stars shine
Brighten the unknown
Capabilities
And one's reach

Support evaporates tears
And straightens crooked eyes
It even curves the most stubborn frown
Into a forever and lasting smile

Support makes time invisible
On your side for keeps sake
Gives the illusion of a 1,460 day journey
To only feel like a mile run you must take

Support spreads to others
Like an infectious or deadly disease
It can be craved like an addiction to an addict
Or a mouse's dependence on cheese
Support is like a bolt to a lock
A link to a chain
Presence is known in light or darkness

111

In time of the unknown or hall of fame

Support resembles the knees
For which my legs stand
Support was delivered to me from you
Whether it was spoken,
thought of or given in hand

I thank you Lord for all of thee
For without support
Like branches to no tree
Before you as a graduate
Strong and tall
Today I would not be

A Christmas Wish
Written December 2005

I wish you a Merry Christmas
And a splendid New Year
To my fellow colleagues that surround me
I wish you good cheer

As the phone rings in the service center From You to You
Think of silver bells
Or jingle bells
One of Santa's favorite tunes

If you get a unique inquiry
You better not pout or cry
Keep smiling
It's not Scrooge
Santa will be watching you and I

When the day is done
Keep caroling
And gliding through the snow
For on this Christmas
I was thinking of you
And I thought that you should know!

A Splinter in my Black Pumps

Inspired by the film Something New
Written September 2006

I must have fallen through the cracks
No, I was not told
I can read your thoughts
They are very cold

I am intelligent
I am capable of thinking
Interpreting and analyzing
Obtaining my degree
Was not a hook up
Or issued just to cut down another tree

I don't think things will get better
And will not hang in there for the team
Support
No demote
Only to promote
Your forever slacking lunch colleague

How am I combative
When I've never raised my voice
The only thing I raised
Was questions about
What you considered I am worth

This question was never
raised directly with you
But to my Lord and Savior

I prayed those days and nights
For your untrustworthy behavior

I am free now from your shackles
In my spirit
Although

My environment is still the same
I will continue to make my climb upward
Your splinters will make me stronger
And it will not make me quit the game

Well Wishes
A wedding gift to newlyweds
Written October 2006

We send you well wishes
As your love grows
Like a seed before it blooms
A lily or a rose

Like a caterpillar
Before it bears
Its wings
Or can fly

These are threads
Of our wishes
For the knot
You will tie

Water, No Ice or Lemon
Written December 2005

My life has refreshed
Much hunger
Much rest

Barriers
Like cubes of ice
Will come
But as a conqueror
It will be overcome

Water, no ice please

Like water
I'm free
Without limitations
Opportunity is all around me

No longer the island
There is land beneath my feet
The bitterness life brings
No longer
Will control the hand it feeds

Water, no lemon please

Thankful for his mercy and grace
Hallelujah
The end
Of this woman's race

Walking and climbing will persist
But weariness has gone away

Weather the storm
The sun is bringing your shine
Your way

Anorexia now gone
Bring forth the silver spoon
Let's feast in the morning
Let's feast in the noon
The fork that tried to slash and cut
Which was made to poke or lift
Is now a torch
Less it's steel
It molds my broken dish

Waiter
I need a napkin please
Like my past
It must unfold

I'm full now
I've dabbed my mouth
Pulled away from the table

You're tip?
Oh
It's the next poem
And the stories
I've told

Seek God
Written February 2006

Expect change
Seek God
Expect persuasion
Seek God

In return
Expect direction
You sought God
Expect understanding
You sought God

Expect continuous blessings

For you
Have
Sought God!

FAITH CORNER

God has blessed me abundantly over the years. He has
delivered me from the darkness of my past and put me
on a new path. He has given me direction, healing, joy,
life, love, a second chance, wisdom—He is the provider of
everything that I need. Oh, how I am rich—in spirit!

Thou wilt shew me the path of life: in thy presence is fullness of joy; at
thy right hand
there are pleasures for evermore.
Psalms 16:11 King James Version (KJV)

But he knoweth the way that I take; when he tried me,
I shall come forth as gold.
Job 23:10 King James Version (KJV)

Are you free from your past hurt, mistakes or disappointments? Have you repented and asked God for forgiveness?

PRAYER CORNER

_____

_____

_____

_____

_____

_____

_____

_____

_____

_____

_____

_____

_____

_____

_____

_____

_____

_____

_____

_____

_____

_____

_____

_____

_____

_____

_____

Amen! Keep the Faith in Jesus Mighty, Powerful & Strong Name!
Next Round!

ROUND 7

UNVEILED
Out of the Closet

What's in Your Closet?

You are the light of the world. A town built on a hill cannot be hidden. Neither do people light a lamp and put it under a bowl. Instead they put it on its stand, and it gives light to everyone in the house. In the same way, let your light shine before others, that they may see your good deeds and glorify your Father in heaven. Matthew 5:14-16 New International Version (NIV)

Well, there you have it! Every piece of the diary is now out from under the bed and out of the closet. I don't know about you, but I thank God for second chances. I also thank Him for grace and mercy, because all of us have been forgiven or provided a second chance for something we didn't even have the sense to repent for before Him.

What's in your closet or in you that God wants to use? We all have a version of *closet sheets*. Some sheets are cotton, while others are silk. Some are 100 thread count; some are 1,000 thread count. Some are crib sheets, while others fit twin beds; some fit king size beds. Some are torn. Some are holey. And know that all sheets will get dirty!

Understand that only God can clean us up and that there is a process and a purpose in what He is doing with your sheets. Accept Jesus as your Lord and Savior, the only way to the father, so you can start a relationship with Him today. And if you did have a relationship with Him before, but somewhere along the way life knocked you down or out or you got injured – don't worry. Stand back up. He's waiting for you too.

SURPRISE! Writing a piece for this last chapter, your FIRST round, is on **YOU**! You don't have to write in the same fashion that I have written. Just let the holy spirit lead you. To help get you started - What are you trusting God to reveal to you in the current round that you are in? In what areas do you need more of God's strength to accomplish goals that align with his will for your life or to remove those things that are not in alignment? Don't know where to begin? Look back and reflect on each of the prayers, that you have written in the previous rounds so far. And if you are still unsure, take it to the corner man. Take it all to God in prayer. I know He will direct your path.

TITLE (Derived from perhaps a memory or specific prayer request)

_____

WRITTEN BY (Your Name)

_____

MONTH/YEAR (Date Completed)

_____

_____

_____

_____

_____

The Whole Armor of God

10 Finally, my brethren, be strong in the Lord and in the power of His might. **11** Put on the whole armor of God, that you may be able to stand against the [b]wiles of the devil. **12** For we do not wrestle against flesh and blood, but against principalities, against powers, against the rulers of [c]the darkness of this age, against spiritual *hosts* of wickedness in the heavenly *places*. **13** Therefore take up the whole armor of God, that you may be able to withstand in the evil day, and having done all, to stand.

14 Stand therefore, having girded your waist with truth, having put on the breastplate of righteousness, **15** and having shod your feet with the preparation of the gospel of peace; **16** above all, taking the shield of faith with which you will be able to quench all the fiery darts of the wicked one. **17** And take the helmet of salvation, and the sword of the Spirit, which is the word of God; **18** praying always with all prayer and supplication in the Spirit, being watchful to this end with all perseverance and supplication for all the saints— **19** and for me, that utterance may be given to me, that I may open my mouth boldly to make known the mystery of the gospel, **20** for which I am an ambassador in chains; that in it I may speak boldly, as I ought to speak. Ephesians 6:10-20 New King James Version (NKJV)

Made in the USA
Middletown, DE
14 December 2022

18544625R00087